To Warren, our grandson, who is a wonderful friend to all.
-L.W.

To Brittany, my sister, who is not only my best friend,
but who has always been there for me.
-L.M.

To all my students, past, present and future.
-J.Y.

Little Lindsey
Makes a Friend

Written by Linda Wagner and Lindsey Moreland

Illustrated by Jodi Youngman

Little Lindsey was four years old when she started going to school. She liked riding to school in her yellow bus most days. She liked her bus driver, Donna, every day.

Little Lindsey liked her classroom most days.

She liked her teacher, Mr. Ryan, every day.

Little Lindsey liked reading and math most days.

She liked the art center every day.

Little Lindsey liked recess and her favorite swing. She liked to sign "more" when she wanted her teacher to give her another push.

Little Lindsey did NOT like recess when someone else was using her favorite swing.

School is a busy place with lots of bright colors and bright lights. School is a noisy place with lots of children and many changes throughout the day.

Little Lindsey didn't like these things very much. Sometimes they made her cry and hide. Little Lindsey has autism which makes her brain understand things in a special way.

Every day Little Lindsey's family would ask her about her school day.

Some days Little Lindsey said, "Ok."

Some days Little Lindsey said, "Not ok."

One day at school a new little boy with blond hair and glasses was swinging on "her" swing. Little Lindsey was **not happy**. She stomped away and walked around the playground for the rest of recess.

"How was your day today?" Little Lindsey's mom asked when she got home.

"Not ok," cried Little Lindsey.

18

Her mom gave her a hug and said, "It's ok. Maybe tomorrow will be better. Let's make eggs."

"Pink eggs?" Little Lindsey asked.

"Yes, let's make pink eggs," her mom answered. So they did.

The next day at school, Little Lindsey went out to recess ready to swing. "Oh no," thought Little Lindsey. The little boy with the blond hair and glasses was swinging on her favorite swing again! She began to cry and ran to hide in the corner of the playground.

Her teacher said, "It's ok. There are three other swings left."

"Not OK," Little Lindsey cried, and she spent the rest of recess hiding and crying.

"How was your day?" Little Lindsey's dad asked when she got home.

"Not ok," said Little Lindsey.

Little Lindsey's dad said, "Maybe tomorrow will be better. Let's go outside and jump on the trampoline." Little Lindsey liked to jump on the trampoline. So they did.

The next day at school, Little Lindsey pushed her way to the front of the recess line. She raced to the swing and got there first.

"Little Lindsey, you cannot budge just to get to the swing first," said her teacher in a kind voice. Little Lindsey did not get to swing on her favorite swing that day. She sat and watched the little boy with the blond hair and glasses swing.

"How was your day?" Little Lindsey's sister Brittany asked.

"Not ok," cried Little Lindsey.

Brittany said, "Maybe tomorrow will be better. Let's put on some music and dance."

Little Lindsey liked music and dancing. So they did.

The next day at school, Little Lindsey **tried** to stay in her spot in the recess line. Once they got outside, she ran to the swing and **almost** got there first, but the little boy with the blond hair and glasses was getting on her favorite swing. She tried not to cry, but she just couldn't help it.

A group of children invited Little Lindsey to play tag. "Not today," she said as she watched the little boy with blond hair and glasses swing.

"Woof woof woof?" Little Lindsey's dog Buddy asked when Little Lindsey got home from school. "Not ok," cried Little Lindsey.

Buddy began spinning in circles chasing his tail. Little Lindsey liked spinning in circles. So they did.

"Maybe tomorrow will be better," she thought.

The next day, Little Lindsey's teacher walked the class outside for recess. Little Lindsey was excited. Her favorite swing was empty. She got on it and began to swing.

The little boy with the blond hair and glasses was swinging on the swing next to her. "Hi, I am Warren. I like to swing, too!" the little boy with the blond hair and glasses said. Little Lindsey answered, "I'm Lindsey."

Little Lindsey's family asked her how her day was when she got home from school.

"How was your day?" They all asked at once.

"Woof, woof, woof?" asked Buddy.

Little Lindsey smiled, "Ok!"

"yeah," they cheered.

The next day at school Little Lindsey saw the little boy with blond hair and glasses in the lunchroom.

"Hi Lindsey," Warren said. "Are you going to swing today?"

"Yes," answered Little Lindsey.

"yeah!" said Warren.

From that day on Little Lindsey went to school each day hoping it would be an "ok" day. Some days it was and some days it wasn't. Sometimes she got her favorite swing and sometimes she did not.

She learned to use the other swings even though they still weren't her favorite. Best of all, she made a new friend which made Little Lindsey happy and proud.

Lindsey Moreland was diagnosed with autism at 28 months old. She faced many challenges in her younger years from getting haircuts, being a picky eater and making friends. Through numerous therapies and outstanding support from others, Lindsey is a successful adult who is not only employed, but also lives independently. Lindsey is an accomplished artist, public speaker and fluent in Spanish. Lindsey has co-authored three other books: Autism: A Family Lives Beyond the Label: The Lindsey Moreland Story, Little Lindsey gets a Haircut, and Little Lindsey is a Picky Eater. Lindsey Moreland is also the illustrator for Koda, the Fluff, gets a Driver's License. Lindsey loves to spend time with her family, cook, and travel.

Linda Wagner is Lindsey Moreland's aunt and an elementary teacher in Wisconsin. She has been teaching for over 25 years. She has worked with many students with special needs and has found that her relationship with Lindsey has helped her be a better teacher for all students. Linda loves working with both Lindsey and Jodi Youngman in this series because they both strive to help others accept and understand differences through their experiences. Linda is a wife, mother, and proud grandmother, dedicating this book to her oldest grandson, Warren Anderson. In her spare time, she enjoys traveling with her husband Mike, hiking and spending time with family.

Jodi Youngman has been an elementary art teacher in Wisconsin since 2005. Through her work in schools, she has been able to work with many students with autism and other special needs. Jodi considered how many people with autism think and created a realistic version of Lindsey. In addition, Jodi aspired and accomplished adding more diversity in this third book in the Little Lindsey series. Accepting others and including others is an important message in this story. Jodi is a wife and mother of three. In her spare time, she enjoys reading, creating art, and spending time with her family. Visit Jodi's website at jodiyoungman.com to learn more.

Be a B.U.D.

(Be Kind, Understand we are all Different, Do the Right Thing.)
By Brittany Moreland, Little Lindsey's sister and best friend

Scan here to visit the Moreland family's website!

I have always had a great relationship with my sister. Growing up with a sister who has autism wasn't always easy, and I often felt like I was on a roller coaster with the ups and downs, twists and turns. However, through it all, Lindsey continues to be an amazing sister and friend. As a child I was diagnosed with and assigned multiple labels including a learning difference, Epilepsy, depression, and an anxiety disorder. I often felt that these challenges made it difficult to make friends. As an adult, I created this acronym to promote being a good friend. Your words matter. Your actions matter. It is time for us all to be a B.U.D. When you are a B.U.D. to others, you not only make a positive difference in someone else's life, but also your own. For more information on the "Be a B.U.D." program go to autismlm.com.

Text Copyright © 2023 by Linda Wagner and Lindsey Moreland
Pictures Copyright © 2023 by Jodi Youngman
All rights reserved. No portion of this book may be reproduced, stored in any electronic system, or transmitted in any form by any means without the written permission of the authors. Brief quotations may be used in literary reviews. All illustration/artwork is the sole copyright of the illustrator.

Printed in the United States of America by IngramSpark
First Printing, 2023

ISBN 978-0-9993488-5-7

IngramSpark
1246 Heil Quarter Blvd.
La Vergne, TN 37086
www.IngramSpark.com

www.ingramcontent.com/pod-product-compliance
Ingram Content Group UK Ltd
Pitfield, Milton Keynes, MK11 3LW, UK
UKRC031609190426
11946UKWH00028B/138